THE SUPERNATURAL KEYS TO A LIFE OF DOMINION

© 2024 Dynamique Ndele

Published by Kingdom Life International Media Library
All rights reserved. No part of this publication may be reproduced, stored in a retrieval system or transmitted in any form or by any means, electronic, mechanical, photocopying, recording or otherwise, without the prior written permission of the copyright owner, with the exception of brief excerpts in magazines, articles, reviews, etc.

For further information or permission, please contact:
Kingdom Life Media Library
PO Box: 3007, Joondalup, WA 6027 Australia
Phone: +61 405133065
Email: kli.joondalup@gmail.com
Website: www.kli.org.au
Cover design by: Dynamique Ndele
Interior design by: Dynamique Ndele
National Library of Australia Cataloguing - in - Publication Data:
Author: Dynamique Ndele Luela –
Title: Supernatural Keys

ISBN: 978-0-6489178-0-9
Subjects: Christian Living / Religious Book
Unless otherwise stated, all Scriptures are taken from the New King James Version (The Holy Bible, New King James Version) Copyright © 1982 by Thomas Nelson, Inc. Used by permission. All rights reserved.

Contents

Chapter 1: The Divine Concept of Dominion.......... 1

Chapter 2: Divine Nature.. 29

Chapter 3: Revelation 43

Chapter 4: Faith.. 53

Chapter 5: Divine Wisdom... 63

Chapter 6: Divine Joy.. 77

Chapter 7: Divine Peace 85

Chapter 8: Understanding Jesus' Supremacy........ 95

Introduction

By creation, Divine nature is embedded in humanity. Created in God's image and likeness, human beings are ambassadors of a heavenly King, a reference point of supernatural realities of the invisible God. Through covenant, those who embrace divine plans on Earth become divine seed germinating into a tree of hope.

Seeds of Abraham are indisputable channels of God's life in earthen vessels. Through supernatural keys, you are being introduced to a company of champions, a groundbreaking Zoe life above limitation, empowered to operate fully in the unseen kingdom.

Able to produce undeniable manifestations in life. These Keys are kingdom equipments that connect to the essence of your purpose while on Earth.

Walking in the spirit of a conqueror is your created destiny. By design, you are a high flyer in the school of dominion, commanding unusual results in every area of your life!

Faith in God rewards. Countless faith generals in the Bible were unshakable in their faith in God. They had their eyes fixed on the reward. God has planned total victory for people of faith. God's intentions for covenant people from the beginning have been a life of total dominion.

Look at the following scriptures in the book of Genesis.

Genesis 1:26 says:

Then God said, "Let Us make man in Our image, according to Our likeness; let them have dominion over the fish of the sea, over the birds of the air, and over the cattle, over all the earth and over every creeping thing that creeps on the earth."

An invisible God created a visible man, placing him over the works of His hands, making him the steward over creation, thus making God King overall in partnership with man on earth. This was joy, pleasure and excitement to the Creator, seeing the created man in charge of divine affairs on earth. To this day the desire to have control is inherent in human hearts.

Regardless of culture, gender, background or social status, all seek to exercise the upper hand over life situations. That is the main motivation behind hard work, sacrifices made in the name of sustaining the family, paying off debts, having a good life, planning for vacations. Humanity is wired with a natural drive toward success. This was natural in the beginning, all creation enjoyed effortless harmony and alignment to the Maker before Satan's interference. Satan's deception of man led to chaos, plunging the entire of human race into the abyss of hopelessness, thus disqualifying man from the original intent of his Maker. We are told in

Genesis 3:4

"Then the serpent said to the woman, "You will not surely die. For God knows that in the day you eat of it your eyes will be opened, and you will be like God, knowing good and evil."

But even before the fall of man, the God of love and wisdom had designed a perfect plan of restoration to reconnect humanity to His original intent by sending His son Jesus Christ. By His death and resurrection, what we lost through rebellion was restored through Christ's obedience on the Cross. In addition, He sent the Holy Spirit to enforce His plan. Anyone adhering to God's plan becomes a son or daughter of the Most High, a qualified recipient of the life of dominion.

But despite divine efforts to rescue humanity, there remain obstacles perpetuated either through ignorance or Satan to keep humanity from stepping into the fullness of the benefits of divine plans. The kingdom of darkness endeavours to keep humanity in ignorance, thus robbing them from the path leading to a fulfilled life made available by God through Jesus Christ of Nazareth.

Walking the path of Calvary leads to a total annihilation of the works of darkness and the demise of all plans of Satan's kingdom. Countless have succumbed to Satan's efforts, demons have successfully convinced the large majority that the concept of the Cross is irrelevant, especially in developed nations, thus relegating the efficiency of the Cross to unlearned and untaught people.

Today, an upsurge of a radical faith globally induced by the God of Heaven is closing the gap significantly. The gospel of the Kingdom is preached without compromise to all the earth, through all means available. Nowadays, the preaching of an uncompromising word of faith crosses boundaries, touches all genders, age groups, nations, and races.

Pointing back to the efficacy and infallibility of the Cross, thus overcoming the plans and strategies of Satan in keeping humanity under a yoke of ignorance. The diabolical plans to rob humanity of God's dream are being exposed. Countless are rediscovering the only road to a better life, JESUS CHRIST.

Every principle I discuss in this book is rooted in who Christ is and what He has done for us on the Cross of Calvary. Reading this book will never benefit you unless you believe in Christ Jesus as the centre of your life, giving Him the total control of your life.

He is the only path leading to a life of dominion. Giving one hundred percent of your life to Christ ensures one hundred percent victory. A good life is God's heartbeat for us, made available only through the person of the Lord Jesus Christ!

John 10:10

> The thief does not come except to steal, and to kill, and to destroy. I have come that they may have life, and that they may have it more abundantly.

1 John 5:4

For whatever is born of God overcomes the world. And this is the victory that has overcome the world–our faith.

When you give your life to Christ, you become born of God, subsequently heir to all the promises of a life of dominion. Supernatural dominion is your covenant heritage and gateway to a life of prosperity and favour. Your enthronement in the spirit, a symbol of honour and dignity. It attracts favour wherever you go. So lay hold of it and let God be magnified in your life in Jesus Christ's name!!

It begins with Jesus. If you want to give your life to Jesus Christ, pray this prayer!!

Lord Jesus Christ, I come to you. I am a sinner, forgive my sins, cleanse me by your precious Blood. I confess Jesus died because of my sin and rose again.

Today, I give my life to you. Fill me with your Holy Spirit, receive me into your kingdom. I believe I am a child of God and I am born again, in Jesus' name. Amen!!

CHAPTER 1

The Divine Concept Of Dominion

Dominion is Your Covenant Heritage

The founder and president of Bahamas Faith Ministries, the late Dr. Myles Munroe, once said: "If the purpose of a thing is not known, abuse is inevitable." You are created for a purpose.

Ignorance of purpose does not cancel it. Discovery of purpose leads to a life of fulfillment and total victory. Your purpose is to dominate!

Attempting to find meaning in earthly materials is the assassin of purpose. Materials did not make you, therefore they don't define you. Your purpose in this life is to have dominion through a relationship with God.

The Almighty is the source of your life and desires. Mortal beings are not to be subjects of your motivation, neither the source of unshakable hope. People fail and change, the Almighty never changes. He devised your purpose, trust Him, love him, depend on Him, follow Him, the only sure path to your purpose, leading unto a place of dominion.

My desire through this book is to lead you to a place of understanding whereby you become comfortable with your purpose. No more tolerating defeat, not another day in your life. Refuse to live at the mercy of your circumstances; you determine the outcome of your life. You are created for dominion in every single area of your life, in your business, in your marriage, in your studies, in your emotions, in your ministry, in all that concerns you.

Why do you get frustrated and angry when you cannot pay your bills, your family is in shambles, your mind in confusion, and there's no progress in your ministry? You despise depending on others to live your life.

You feel drained, hopeless when you are stuck in debt with no means to pay it back. Anything that overrules you wears you down because it opposes your natural make up. You are wired a dominator!

A person who enjoys depending on others all the time displays signs of dysfunction.

Embedded in you is a spiritual fabric that resembles God's nature. God created you. He longs for you to tailor your life after Him. Be partakers of His Divine nature that knows no defeat or boundaries.

The nature of God qualifies you to be self-sufficient, creative, successful and progressive, because of the Spirit of dominion! That is why you must learn how to dominate over emotions, feelings, opposition, fears, phobias, greed, or anything that seeks to enslave you. Embrace and practice divine concepts pertaining to dominion.

What is dominion and its covenant purpose?

Is mastery, total control, pre-eminence, being in charge, having the last word, having an upper-hand, dominating

Genesis 1:26 says

And God said, Let us make man in our image, after our likeness: and let them have dominion over the fish of the sea, and over the fowl of the air, and over the cattle, and over all the earth, and over every creeping thing that creeps upon the earth.

The earth is full of cruelties. You hear of daily injustices, racism, xenophobia, sexism everywhere. Millions are oppressed, used, not given equal opportunities. Poor workers of Third World countries are exploited of their produce by rich countries failing to compete in international markets. Unfair regulations set in place forbid equal access to wealth.

How can we break free from such great obstacles and soar higher in this life in face of such great odds? The key is in the respect of the covenant of dominion.

What you respect increases in you.

Psalms 74:20 says

Have respect to the covenant; For the dark places of the earth are full of the haunts of cruelty.

The covenant of dominion infuses you with divine might to defeat the cruelty of the dark places of the earth, living your life fully and unhindered. Through the covenant of dominion, you operate on divine frequency.

Psalms 8:3

When I consider Your heavens, the work of Your fingers, The moon and the stars, which You have ordained, What is man that You are mindful of him, And the son of man that You visit him? For You have made him a little lower than the angels, And You have crowned him with glory and honor. You have made him to have dominion over the works of Your hands; You have put all things under his feet, All sheep and oxen–Even the beasts of the field, The birds of the air, And the fish of the sea that pass through the paths of the seas.

God crowned Adam and Eve with glory and gave them dominion.

Dominion is divine glory in operation. Once you understand the mystery of divine glory, you will operate in fullness of dominion. Dominion is the manifestation of divine glory over you.

You don't need to seek dominion; you live in it through divine glory. Chasing after success and fulfillment without glory is like a dog chasing its own tail or a person chasing his own shadow. You become wearied and all invested efforts have no value. God's success finds its roots in dominion flowing from divine glory.

Sadly, countless seek dominion while ignoring the root of it all. Years ago the Lord began to teach me about dominion. Through Scriptures I understood the Lord's desire for humanity was total dominion on Earth. This I preached and taught everywhere, I organised conferences and several meetings around the same subject. Nevertheless the results were limited. In some cases there were no results at all. I began to question the reasons behind my failures. The Lord began to enlighten me and redirect my focus. Wrong perception breeds negative results. When I shifted my focus all changed.

The Glory of God

In this book I do not intend to delve into the subject of glory, but rather how I personally became a recipient of this great dimension by grace. I simply desire to acquaint you with it.

Understanding divine glory has changed my life completely and my reading of Scriptures. I have resolved to make the glory the purpose of my life, the delight and joy of my ministry. The glory of God cannot be fully explained, the glory of God is the fullness of who God is and all He possesses. How can a mortal being fully understand and explain the fullness of immortal God and His possessions? Though all that has been revealed to us in Christ, in this life we experience a fragment of the unsearchable wisdom of the immortal and eternal God.

1 Corinthians 13:9 For we know in part and we prophesy in part

What is the glory of God?

The glory of God is the manifestation of His presence. God is omnipresent, meaning everywhere, but the manifestation of His Presence is conditional. Intentionally Creating the environment is necessary to experience the manifestation of His presence.

God is Holy, He dwells in praise, is the God of faith and much more when you understand His conducive environment, He is bound to manifest Himself.

Psalms 22:3 But You are holy, Enthroned in the praises of Israel.

1 Peter 1:16 because it is written, "Be holy, for I am holy."

Realm of Tangibility

Exodus 16:6-7 Then Moses and Aaron said to all the children of Israel, "At evening you shall know that the Lord has brought you out of the land of Egypt. And in the morning you shall see the glory of the Lord; for He hears your complaints against the Lord. But what are we, that you complain against us?

In response to the complaints of Israel, Moses and Aaron told the people that they would see the glory, for God heard their complaints. I thought it would have rained fire, thunder, lightning or they would have seen the cloud over them. Yet Moses began to expound on the meat and bread that the people would eat. Were meat and bread the glory of God? Moses and Aaron called manna, glory. A substance that could be touched and eaten.

Exodus 16:6-8

Then Moses and Aaron said to all the children of Israel, "At evening you shall know that the Lord has brought you out of the land of Egypt. And in the morning you shall see the glory of the Lord; for He hears your complaints against the Lord. But what are we, that you complain against us?" Also Moses said, "This shall be seen when the Lord gives you meat to eat in the evening, and in the morning bread to the full; for the Lord hears your complaints which you make against Him. And what are we? Your complaints are not against us but against the Lord."

When Jesus changed water into wine, it was called glory.

John 2:10

And he said to him, "Every man at the beginning sets out the good wine, and when the guests have well drunk, then the inferior. You have kept the good wine until now!

When you live in the glory you walk in the tangibility of the supernatural. In the glory, the immaterial becomes concrete, a confession turns into a manifestation.

One day while driving in Sydney, Australia, the Spirit whispered in my heart that these are days of glory!

I heard it clearly and as I pondered the idea, I concluded the Lord desired that I teach it. During that time, I pioneered a church in Sydney, it was the first year. The church was very small and I was still learning my way around Sydney, having come from a different city, Melbourne. I began to teach on the glory of God. Scripturally, I understood glory to be a realm of tangibility, that when you speak of the glory, manifestations take place. That was not my experience, in fact the opposite was true.

I saw no glory results. One day I was invited by a friend who hosted Barry Thornley, also known as the glory man. I witnessed an amazing reality of God's glory. After his teaching, pastor Barry asked everyone to stand up to pray for the glory to be manifested. This I had never seen in my entire life. After a short prayer he asked every single person to check on their hands. Suddenly out of nowhere, people began to drip with oil gold dust.

After the service I spoke to Pastor Barry and later we became good friends. After a while I invited him to my meetings. He came and the same thing happened. I will never forget the Indian church where the glory came as a cloud of gold dust raining down, covering the floor. They needed a bucket to sweep the place up after the service. I felt like I had found the hidden pearl; I was ready to sell everything to buy the field. One day Pastor Barry ministered at a friend's church. At the end of the service, the church floor was covered with diamonds - I mean DIAMONDS!!! The members picked up over twenty diamonds.

I have seen healings, words of knowledge, and several supernatural manifestations through the glory meetings with Pastor Barry. Little did I know every time

Pastor Barry prayed for me, I received an impartation of the same grace.

Now by the grace of God, everywhere I go, the same grace is manifested. Glory to God! Some don't understand it, others disregard it, but I treasure it; ever since then my life has changed for good.

In the acknowledgment of his recent book on glory invasion Pastor Barry has mentioned the impartation of the glory grace I received through his prayers. Thank God for such great men who dare to live on the edge. I have had countless experiences with Pastor Barry that have changed my theology for good. Today by God's grace and mercy, everywhere I go I pray and command the manifestation of divine glory and it happens. I know it will always happen.

I know some readers might ask how can you command the presence of God and see its manifestation?

Isaiah 45:11

Thus says the Lord, The Holy One of Israel, and his Maker: "Ask Me of things to come concerning My sons; And concerning the work of My hands, you command Me."

One day I was in Dallas, Fort Worth. I wondered about the same thing, the Lord led me to.

Habakkuk 2:14.

For the earth will be filled with the knowledge of the glory of the Lord, As the waters cover the sea.

As I studied this portion of Scripture I realized that the word knowledge in Habakkuk, among the several meanings, also means science. Do you know that science is predictable? While I read this portion of scripture I was in the USA, getting ready to return to Australia. I knew without a shadow of doubt how many hours it would take me to get back home. I sat on the plane with confidence, being ensured that the plane would take off and land according to the time announced. The plane functions according to scientific principle, so its operation is predictable. What the Lord was trying to tell me was the earth will be filled with the knowledge of divine glory as science, meaning it will be predictable. Why not? Gone are the days where we wondered about God's manifestation.

Divine Goodness or Glory

Exodus 33:18-19

18 And he said, "Please, show me Your glory." Then He said, "I will make all My goodness pass before you, and I will proclaim the name of the Lord before you. I will be gracious to whom I will be gracious, and I will have compassion on whom I will have compassion."

Moses asked to see divine glory; the Lord responded with His goodness. The goodness of God, as defined by Nehemiah, are houses, vineyards, cisterns already dug, olive groves, fruit trees in abundance. It is imperative to produce tangible results as we embark on a glory journey. David goes further to explain that goodness and mercy follow us; these are not static but dynamic realities, in motion, tangible and alive.

Nehemiah 9:25

And they took strong cities and a rich land, And possessed houses full of all goods, Cisterns already dug, vineyards, olive groves, And fruit trees in abundance. So they ate and were filled and grew fat, And delighted themselves in Your great goodness. Nehemiah calls strong cities, rich land, houses full of goods, cisterns ,vineyards, olive groves, fruits tree in abundance,

The prophetic word of Isaiah is a revelation of divine glory, empowering covenant people for a life of dominion at the rise of darkness in their generation. Glory is at its best in darkness; when chaos visits us, the glory shows up. The earth is a perfect place for the glory. The darker it gets, the more glorious we become. These are the best days to be alive. Darkness is everywhere. We should rule and reign in this life through divine glory.

Isaiah 60:2-3 says:

For behold, the darkness shall cover the earth, And deep darkness the people; But the Lord will arise over you, And His glory will be seen upon you. The Gentiles shall come to your light, And kings to the brightness of your rising.

The Almighty desires to fill the earth with His glory, His manifested presence, unleashing the potent forces of His divine abilities to His covenant people. His manifested presence equips you for an unprecedented life of total dominion.

The manifestation of God's presence in the last days is subject to His divine agenda. This encapsulates the only seed of hope for the days ahead in a troubled world. When I was in the USA, a pastor asked me to preach for him. As I waited on the Lord, He showed me He keeps the best for last. The best wine was kept for last at a Cana feast; when released, it brought joy and fulfillment. This wine is the only remedy for the joy of the human heart in these last days.

Apostle Paul, in his second letter to Timothy in chapter 3, emphasized the impossibilities that will face the people of the last days. The apostle used the word perilous, meaning times beyond human capacity and preparedness. Apart from Divine glory, none is prepared to face the challenges ahead of us. Because of His love for us, the Master has reserved the greater glory for the last days to prepare covenant people to be in charge despite the changing times and seasons. We are, of all generations, the most blessed!

2 Timothy 3

But know this, that in the last days perilous times will come

No matter your location on this planet, there will be little or no hope for significant changes in your world apart from divine glory. Nowadays wickedness is rampant, increasing exponentially, of which Jesus the Lord said: "When the Son of Man comes, will he find faith on the earth?"

Luke 18:8 I tell you that He will avenge them speedily. Nevertheless, when the Son of Man comes, will He really find faith on the earth?"

When I was in Queensland, Australia, three young Christian men visited me in my hotel room very worried and wondering if they would succeed in their Christian walk, seeing the increase of vileness today!

A young married Christian man came to me and dropped to his knees, wanting prayer over the lasciviousness of his sexual life with prostitutes.

Evil is arising, but thank God for His glory. The greater the darkness, the brighter the glory. As you operate in your covenant of dominion, you set the rules and your reality becomes independent of your society. His manifested presence shields you from the decadency of your society.

Moses was given the choice to move to the Promised Land without God's presence; he refused. What was it about the Lord's presence that Moses was prepared to endure the scorching heat of the desert with it, rather than the Promised Land without it?

God's presence brings the manifestation of His fullness, regardless of the situation, His presence transforms the environment to be conformed to His glorious nature. His presence is the pearl of great price that when found, a man sold all he had to purchase it. Your height in the life of dominion depends on the magnitude of His presence over your life. Little presence, little dominion. No presence, no dominion.

Exodus 33:15 says:

Then he said to Him, "If Your Presence does not go with us, do not bring us up from here.

When you value His presence beyond any convenience, you become a candidate for glory school. Every time Israel valued His presence they enjoyed the fruits of the land, but when they despised His presence, they lived at the mercy of the enemy.

Determine to stay in His presence, by making His word the standard of your life. In God's presence your future is guaranteed. Your worst nightmare with God is better than worldly wealth without Him. The presence of God is the key factor to an ever expanding and growing life of dominion through the power of His glory.

Matthew 13:46

Who, when he had found one pearl of great price, went and sold all that he had and bought it

Psalm 84:10 For a day in Your courts is better than a thousand.

I would rather be a doorkeeper in the house of my God Than dwell in the tents of wickedness.

Determining Factor of Dominion

Dominion is rooted in divine nature and character. The Almighty is lofty, beyond the realm of human abilities. The Almighty is so High that Prophet Isaiah declared: "I saw the Lord high and lifted up and his train filled the temple."

A man asked a Christian friend, "Why are you so successful and happy?" He responded, "I can't help it! Walking with the Lord sets you on high places." Believers in Christ are born from above through the covenant of Calvary. Your citizenship is above. Today if someone asks what your country of origin is, boldly respond above!

He who comes from above is above all, you are from above so you are above all. While I was in South Africa, someone with an African passport asked me why I could travel freely around the world without the stress of the visa, while he struggled. I responded, "It is not my fault I am an Australian citizen!"

If you are in need, you need the Almighty! I discovered if I know Him then I don't need to beg men.

John 3:31 He who comes from above is above all; he who is of the earth is earthly and speaks of the earth. He who comes from heaven is above all.

Today, decide to cut the umbilical cord that feeds your dependence on people. Walk in the light of the Almighty, His nature and character, and you will conquer. Know this! What God can't do, can't be done.

I used to be the biggest people pleaser - I would risk anything to please others. Then I discovered I don't need anybody but the Almighty. Love people but depend on the Almighty. This is liberating!!

Remember! People manipulate you when they know you need them. Abraham said to the king of Salem, "I will receive nothing from you lest you say I made Abraham rich." He who makes you can break you.

Genesis 14:23

That I will take nothing, from a thread to a sandal strap, and that I will not take anything that is yours, lest you should say, 'I have made Abram rich.

You are not a liability, you are an asset from above. Trust the Almighty! Resolve to have total dependence on the invisible God. If the Almighty can't help you, then you don't need help. If the Almighty can't give to you, you don't need it. Understanding the value of your citizenship sets you apart from your generation. You have not manifested your divinity until the mention of your name breeds jealousy and controversy in your generation. Through His manifested Presence, you are bound to shine.

Psalm 34:5 says

They looked to Him and were radiant, And their faces were not ashamed.

I see you shining in Jesus Name!!!

CHAPTER 2

Divine Nature

The Almighty God is the God of Abraham, Isaac and Jacob, a covenant keeper. The sovereign King of righteousness, King of glory, King of kings, Lord of lords, all sufficient, the Wellspring of wisdom and life.

His names are an avenue to a deeper revelation of His nature and character. El

Elyon is the Most High God, not having a beginning or an end. Did not begin in the beginning; began the beginning. He is the source of dominion and well-spring of conquest.

The patriarchs drank from His well and dominated. Through Him, Abraham defeated four kings with three hundreds and eighteen men, home-trained! This God is a Spirit. He created you like Him, so you are a spirit being, but you live in a body. Your dominion is a product of your spirituality. You are the fruits of His loins, your divinity is anchored in His nature, knowing Him as the source of your dominion.

Man is both created and formed, but God did not give dominion to the formed man, but the created man, the spirit of God's image.

Genesis 1:26

Then God said, "Let Us make man in Our image, according to Our likeness; let them have dominion over the fish of the sea, over the birds of the air, and over the cattle, over all the earth and over every creeping thing that creeps on the earth.

John 4:24

God *is* Spirit, and those who worship Him must worship in spirit and truth.

Genesis 2:7

And the Lord God formed man *of* the dust of the ground, and breathed into his nostrils the breath of life; and man became a living being.

Exodus 6:3

I appeared to Abraham, to Isaac, and to Jacob, as God Almighty, but by my name Lord I was not known to them.

Abraham, Isaac, Jacob and Moses connected to the same God, yet each had a fresh revelation. Each one's perception depended on his encounter with God. How do you know Him? As your Healer, as your Provider, as your Protector? Until you establish your revelation of God, something will always shake you in life's crises. It is hard to trust and follow a person you don't know.

A friend advised me to stop focusing on Divine manifestation and instead preach the word only. I responded, "If I stop trusting God for manifestation, I will stop preaching. I know Him as the God of manifestation!"

2 Peter 1:3-4 says

As His divine power has given to us all things that pertain to life and godliness, through the knowledge of Him who called us by glory and virtue, by which have been given to us exceedingly great and precious promises, that through these you may be partakers of the divine nature, having escaped the corruption that is in the world through lust.

Divine nature is the gateway to a life of total dominion; the master key to life's impediments and obstructions. Divine nature delivers life's precious delicacies to you without sweat. It provides a platform for victories and distinction on the battlefield of life. It enables you to eat the good of the land and inherit the labour of the wicked. Through divine nature, you are no longer a commoner.

Divine nature breaks the stronghold of carnal limitation, propelling you to your place of dominion. It causes you to triumph over diabolical manoeuvres designed to trap and destroy you. Through Divine nature, you access the fullness of divine power commanding and defeating the cohorts of hell.

Regeneration Through the Incorruptible Seed

You are born of God through the incorruptible seed, which is God's Word, having placed your faith in Christ's finished work. Through Divine seed, His Word. You are regenerated in your spirit, qualified for a perfect, harmonious relationship with Almighty God by the power of His Holy Spirit.

You are a qualified recipient of Divine promises, making you an heir of Divine nature. God delights to share His nature with you, making you a Possessor of the earth with faithful Abraham. Through Divine Nature, you enter the world of exploits and join a great cloud of witnesses proclaiming the certainty of divine faithfulness.

We are gods!! Someone said you cannot say that! Why not? God is the Lord of all things. He suffers no identity crisis, neither is He insecure. God knows He is El Elyon. None will ever beat Him. He has no problem sharing His nature with us, His children.

Psalms 82:6

I said, "You are gods, and all of you are children of the Most High.

Covenant power of divine knowledge

Hosea 4:6 states:

My people are destroyed for lack of knowledge. Because you have rejected knowledge, I also will reject you from being priest for Me; Because you have forgotten the law of your God, I also will forget your children.

Have you ever heard a saying: "Sticks and stone may break my bones but words will never hurt me."? Nothing can be further from the truth. Ignorance kills!

Words are containers of thought creating your world. Your divine nature is made available to you through the knowledge of the Word. Divine knowledge is the doorway to His Nature, unlocking the virtue of His power for dominion. The knowledge of the Most High is reachable through His Word.

Do not be ignorant, know His Word, believe His Word, speak His Word, think His Word; the Word is the cradle of Divine knowledge and qualifies you for an unhindered life of exploits.

Daniel 11:32 says:

Those who do wickedly against the covenant he shall corrupt with flattery; but the people who know their God shall be strong, and carry out great exploits.

Divine knowledge empowers you to soar on wings of triumph, sets you in charge over the affairs of life, and makes you a point of reference. Daniel dominated and ruled Babylon through Divine knowledge. The King demanded that only the God of Daniel was to be worshipped. Through Divine Knowledge, you become a ruler and centre of wisdom.

Divine Knowledge illuminates your spirit. Once you determine to be a lover of His Word, and make the Knowledge of the Most High your delight, you will grow in the light of His nature. You will break and pierce through the curtain of demonic limitations that imposes darkness and veils human minds; you will expand your influence in the arena of human affairs. Your elevation is the Heavenly Father's joy as co-sharers of His nature. You are the carrier of Divine fragrance everywhere you go through the virtue of His Word.

2 Corinthians 2:14

Now thanks be to God who always leads us in triumph in Christ, and through us diffuses the fragrance of His knowledge in every place.

You represent His dominion and His excellence everywhere. As He is, so you are in this world. Divine knowledge is infused with covenant power for believers. This same power raised Jesus from the dead. It will raise you from the dust of misery and cause you to become a champion. You become a commander and a liberating force for the oppressed.

1 John 4:17

Love has been perfected among us in this: that we may have boldness in the day of judgment; because as He is, so are we in this world.

Romans 8:11

But if the Spirit of him who raised Jesus from the dead dwells in you, he who raised Christ from the dead will also give life to your mortal bodies through his Spirit who dwells in you.

Eighteen years ago, I was diagnosed with Hepatitis C; I did not have a full understanding of this ailment. But I understood I was a partaker of His divine nature, through the light of the Word. I knew I was one with Him because of the finished work of Calvary, subsequently everything that He is, I am. Thus, anything that happens to me must reflect the fullness of His nature, character, and integrity. My doctor advised me to learn how to live with it. However, after an intense time with the Word of God, I realised I was already healed 2000 years ago.

I refused to believe Christ in me would enjoy sharing the same room with a Hepatitis C virus. I refuted that concept with everything in me. The Bible teaches the believer becomes one with the Lord through faith.

I deduced, Christ could not be a Hep C carrier, so why would I? I went to the Word again and again. After around three weeks, the Word killed Hepatitis C.

Today I am Hepatitis C free. Glory to God! It is God's heartbeat for you to walk in the reality of this covenant of honour, lifting you above the predicament of man and the limitation of the flesh.

You might not have your expectation as yet, but if you can see it in the Word, you can see it in your world. Get understanding and manifest Divine nature through you.

1 Corinthians 6:17

But he who is joined to the Lord is one spirit with Him

CHAPTER 3

Revelation

Revelation is the unfolding of Divine mysteries to a hungry and open heart, the removal of cover from the blindness of human limitation while providing insight into the realm of Divine. Through revelation, God empowers you to walk in the fullness of dominion, having your spiritual light lit above ordinary people.

Revelation changes the frequency by which you operate from terrestrial to celestial, from zero to hero. From depravity to dominion. It releases the full force of the divine Word and propels you to a life of total dominion.

Once you become committed to live in the realm of divine revelation, you unlock the full potential of Divinity in you and are in control of human affairs.

Psalms 119:130 says

The entrance of Your words gives light; it gives understanding to the simple.

Light dominates darkness, it brings clarity and distinction. Light dictates your direction. Once a dark room is illuminated, the direction also is made available. Every limitation in your life can be traced back to the lack of light.

Light moves you from the ordinary to the extraordinary. The amount of light you carry in your spirit man will determine how far you operate in your divinity and rise in the school of dominion. Light releases you in the realm of Divine and makes you a commander in life. You must allow the Holy Spirit to inject Divine light into your spirit through meditation of his Word.

Divinity Through Divine Revelation

John 10:35 says:

If He called them gods, to whom the word of God came (and the Scripture cannot be broken),

When the Word becomes revelation or Rhema, it births a living faith into your heart leading you to divine manifestation and giving you mastery over that light. And it makes you a god over your situations.

Moses became a god to Pharaoh; he influenced Egyptian life in every area. He was an agent of deliverance.

A revelation received at the backside of a desert stopped four hundred and thirty years of slavery. Your current location does not matter. Get revelation; you will be promoted and the world will hear from you.

Exodus 7:1

> So the Lord said to Moses: "See, I have made you as God to Pharaoh, and Aaron your brother shall be your prophet.

Stop seeking for human connection - seek revelation. It is your gateway to the world of greatness. Get light and you will stop the calamity in your life. It changes your habitation. Through divine revelation David, once shepherd, later lived in a palace. Once your habitation changes, your living conditions change.

I was born in central Africa, then moved to Australia; my life has changed completely by changing my habitation. Change your habitation from the written Word to divine revelation.

That is where divine secrets of covenant people are released. Light makes the supernatural accessible when the need arises. It creates an atmosphere where angelic beings operate. Light attracts the resources needed to finish your journey. You don't have to look at your abilities and relationships to determine how you'll finish. Walk in the light. God Has made His Unlimited kingdom supplies available to the enlightened.

Just like the moon needs the sun in order to shine, so you need divine light. God is light, He dominates all. Pledge allegiance to walk in His light. In His light, you will have light.

Psalm 36:9

For with You is the fountain of life; In Your light we see light.

Revelation born out of the divine word manifests divine glory. Relationship with God's word breeds revelation. Once revelation invades your heart, your spirit is illuminated; that's the key to dominion.

The Holy Spirit is a life giving Spirit. He sheds light on God's word. The letter kills, but the Spirit gives life. Your connection with Him floods light into the spirit man, causing the word to leap from logos to Rhema.

Luke 2:32 says

A light to bring revelation to the Gentiles, And the glory of Your people Israel."

Spirit of Light

Genesis 1:1-3 says

In the beginning God created the heavens and the earth. 2 The earth was without form, and void; and darkness was on the face of the deep. And the Spirit of God was hovering over the face of the waters. 3 Then God said, "Let there be light"; and there was light.

God spoke under the influence of the Holy Spirit. He transformed Divine confession to manifestation. Jesus spoke the Word of Spirit and life. Without knowing the Holy Spirit, you will never receive light from above. The Holy Spirit is the light source in the kingdom of God; get your light from Him. His light conquers darkness, birthing dominion.

He leads in fullness, even when you are surrounded by confusion. The Holy Spirit knows how to instruct your heart by flooding it with Divine light, piercing any hindering force. The Holy Spirit knows how to direct your soul to the light that will profit you. Trust Him, follow Him, rely on Him, depend on Him, with Him dominion is inevitable. He is the sure path of the kingdom's dominion. Life does not answer to luck but to light. Your destiny is tied to light, get light, and live in dominion.

In the kingdom of God, your light determines your height. Divine revelation determines the quality of your life on Earth. There is no partiality in the kingdom. Your age, your gender, your background, the colour of your skin, your status, your education are of no consequence. None is responsible for the quality of your life but you.

Get the light and change your world. The story of the prodigal son is the best example of how God's light can impact and change your life. The prodigal son knew he had an inheritance and was a qualified recipient of the father's substances. Though he squandered his portion, he knew his father had more than enough.

He moved from the pig den to the palace through the emergence of light. No matter where you are now, Divine light is the answer to your challenges, you can be set in motion and defeat what handicaps you to enjoy your life. You can be victorious!!

The greatest light in the kingdom is the person, Jesus Christ. Through Him, you access His light giver, the Holy Spirit.

Darkness does not comprehend this light. The word comprehend simply means darkness cannot handle, overcome or defeat this light. The light of Christ that floods your soul is a nightmare to the kingdom of darkness. Once the light of the person of Jesus lands in the womb of your heart, darkness becomes powerless.

John 1:5

And the light shines in the darkness, and the darkness did not comprehend it.

Isaiah 48:17

Thus says the Lord, your Redeemer, The Holy One of Israel: "I am the Lord your God, Who teaches you to profit, Who leads you by the way you should go.

CHAPTER 4

Faith

Bible faith is a spiritual force fuelling the human spirit for a life of conquest. Faith is a stronghold on the battlefield of life. It triumphs over all, everywhere. Demonic forces, or man's tradition, can not inhibit the forces of faith.

It is the currency of heaven. Heaven opens its gate to faith and releases without condition to its demands. Jesus could not resist the faith of a non-covenant woman who demanded a miracle out of season.

Jesus had to deal with double disqualification in a woman demanding a miracle. He was not yet ready to perform a miracle, and the woman was Syro-Phoenician, the woman of faith bombarded heaven with fire faith. Heavenly gates were opened, and she received her heart's desires. A miracle was performed out of season in response to stubborn Syro-Phoenician faith.

Many people wait for God's timing. God's timing is faith dictated. Your divine time is now, because faith is now! Mary, the mother of Jesus, received a miracle out of season. Faith dictates the time!

Matthew 15:20-28

And behold, a woman of Canaan came from that region and cried out to Him, saying, "Have mercy on me, O Lord, Son of David!

My daughter is severely demon-possessed." But He answered her not a word. And His disciples came and urged Him, saying, "Send her away, for she cries out after us." But He answered and said, "I was not sent except to the lost sheep of the house of Israel. Then she came and worshiped Him, saying, "Lord, help me!" But He answered and said, "It is not good to take the children's bread and throw it to the little dogs." And she said, "Yes, Lord, yet even the little dogs eat the crumbs which fall from their master's table. Then Jesus answered and said to her, "O woman, great is your faith! Let it be to you as you desire." And her daughter was healed from that very hour.

John 2:4

Jesus said to her, "Woman, what does your concern have to do with Me? My hour has not yet come.

Hebrews 11:1

Now faith is the substance of things hoped for, the evidence of things not seen

Even if you are in the midst Gods timing, you still need faith to unlock Heaven, so get faith. Faith levels the playing field for all; no excuse for failure. Faith is a common denominator and main thread for people who desire dominion. Faith is a remedy against envy and jealousy. God said to Cain, If you do well, you will be accepted. The Almighty is just. He is not a respecter of person, but of faith. Live by faith and you will walk in the fullness of your dominion.

Faith is a seed born out of divine revelation encapsulated in the Word of God. Is the master key to the world of exploit. You cannot experience the conquering force of faith until it is planted in your heart.

Faith is not a theology, a movement or a Christian confession. It releases the spiritual potential of the divine word planted in your heart as a seed, causes the word planted in the soil of your heart to grow until you receive your full expectation. Faith cannot unleash its potent force if the divine seed of the Word remains unplanted.

You become a living wonder and the master in life by becoming a conscious Word Sower in the light of faith. Through faith, you have access to God's voice, making you a champion and commander in life. Through faith, you have access to a world of unlimited possibilities. It is the only kingdom factor that responds and conquers the impossible.

Faith gives you access to a life of unlimited possibilities, positions you to live as a commander in life and anchors you as a kingdom heir. The Word planted manifests through faith. Through faith, your life becomes a city of refuge where provisions are found for many.

By faith, you access the shadow of the Almighty and enjoy divine company. Every Bible general was staunch in the school of faith, for nothing can withstand the authority of faith.

Genesis 4:7

If you do well, will you not be accepted? And if you do not do well, sin lies at the door. And its desire *is* for you, but you should rule over it.

Mark 4:14

The Sower sows the word.

Hebrews 11 states

By faith Abraham, when he was tested, offered up Isaac, and he who had received the promises offered up his only begotten son, of whom it was said, "In Isaac your seed shall be called," concluding that God was able to raise him up, even from the dead, from which he also received him in a figurative sense. By faith Isaac blessed Jacob and Esau concerning things to come. By faith Jacob, when he was dying, blessed each of the sons of Joseph, and worshiped, leaning on the top of his staff. By faith Joseph, when he was dying, made mention of the departure of the children of Israel, and gave instructions concerning his bones. By faith Moses, when he was born, was hidden three months by his parents, because they saw he was a beautiful child; and they were not afraid of the king's command. By faith Moses, when he became of age, refused to be called the son of Pharaoh's daughter, choosing rather to suffer affliction with the people of God than to enjoy the passing pleasures of sin, esteeming the reproach of Christ greater riches than the treasures in Egypt; for he looked to the reward. By faith he forsook Egypt, not fearing the wrath of the king; for he endured as seeing Him who is invisible. By faith he kept the Passover and the sprinkling of blood, lest he who destroyed the firstborn should touch them. By faith they passed through the Red Sea as by dry land, whereas the Egyptians, attempting to do so, were drowned.

Matthew 19:26 says:

But Jesus looked at them and said to them, "With men this is impossible, but with God all things are possible."

Mark 9:23

Jesus said to him, "If you can believe, all things are possible to him who believes."

Faith elevates you to God's class. Matthew says: "All things are possible with God." Mark says: "If you can believe, all things are possible." Get faith from His Word, plant it in the soil of your heart, guard it against the enemy of your progress, and you are set for a life of dominion.

Faith is your currency to the world of exploits. God is a covenant keeper. He is the Lord of legality. Your heart's desires must be grounded in the legal document, His Word.

My mum, in her difficult times, would pray, "Lord, remember me, for I have ten children." I did not know then, or else I would have said to her, "Mama, stop wasting your time and God's. He is not listening!"

Your situation, good or bad, is not the basis for divine response. God responds to the spoken word mixed with faith. I was in India and Africa and I saw great poverty. If needs were the basis of divine response, there would not be any poverty on the planet. He responds to His Word.

Jeremiah 1:11-12

Then the Lord said to me, "You have seen well, for I am ready to perform My word."

Isaiah 55:11

So shall My word be that goes forth from My mouth; It shall not return to Me void, But it shall accomplish what I please, And it shall prosper in the thing for which I sent it.

Find a Word tailored and designed to the specificity of your circumstances and stand on it. If you need finances, health, breakthrough or others, seek for these Scriptures. I wrote a book, God's Promises for Your Kingdom Inheritance. This is not a book, but a compilation of divine promises, from Genesis to Revelation. I wrote this hoping to help those seeking to get the promises of God for their situations.

CHAPTER 5

Divine Wisdom

Proverbs 3:19

The Lord by wisdom founded the earth; By understanding He established the heavens;

Wisdom was present before the foundation of the world. God gave dominion after the world was created, which means wisdom is ancient, greater than dominion. If you walk in wisdom, you are fastened to the ancient root of all things. Wisdom is the ability to apply knowledge.

Knowledge is acquired, but wisdom is given. Wisdom is God's commodity for the elevation of covenant people. It distinguishes your life and makes you a champion. It guarantees the flow of divine ideas that catapult you to a life of dignity and significance.

Wisdom is the key factor to becoming uncommon and living a life exceeding the achievement of your generation. It guarantees the manifestation of divine ideas which break any limitation of the human mind.

Wisdom is the key factor in sweatless victory. It is the only sure building agent. Only through wisdom will your legacy outlive you. The earth is the canvas where God painted all His desires. Without wisdom, you have no foundation and are doomed to fail.

Wisdom anchors your dream and gives you hope for a lasting legacy. Your ability to walk in the fullness of God's covenant is woven into the accessibility of Divine wisdom. Without wisdom, your efforts are wasted and your investments become enemy assets.

Proverbs 9

Wisdom has built her house, She has hewn out her seven pillars; She has slaughtered her meat, She has mixed her wine, She has also furnished her table. She has sent out her maidens, She cries out from the highest places of the city,"Whoever is simple, let him turn in here!"As for him who lacks understanding, she says to him,"Come, eat of my bread and drink of the wine I have mixed. Forsake foolishness and live, and go in the way of understanding.

Someone once said if you cannot beat them, join them. Wisdom has already built her house. Do you want to build? Do you want to achieve? Whatever you need, wisdom has already done it. Join her. Wisdom is divinely engineered for your total dominion. You become a pacesetter and a consultant above your peers. It sets you apart and causes you to excel. Wisdom empowers you to rule over the enemy.

The forces of wisdom break the hindering forces of darkness and empower you to soar with wings of an eagle. Solomon chose wisdom over wealth, army victory over his enemy. He was the wisest man on earth; he chose wisdom. In return, he owned the wealth of the known world.

Whatever is not born of wisdom will never defeat the wiles and the strategies of the enemy. Divine wisdom commands angelic attraction, releasing heavenly fragrance able to expel all demonic activities. The presence of wise men in Joseph's life triggered angelic dreams. Get wisdom today!

Matthew 2:13

When the Wise Men had left, Joseph had a dream. In the dream an angel of the Lord appeared to him. "Get up!" the angel said. "Take the child and his mother and escape to Egypt. Stay there until I tell you to come back. Herod is going to search for the child. He wants to kill him."

The mystery of wisdom

Job 28:12-28

But where can wisdom be found? And where is the place of understanding? Man does not know its value, Nor is it found in the land of the living. The deep says, 'It is not in me'; And the sea says, 'It is not with me.' It cannot be purchased for gold, Nor can silver be weighed for its price. It cannot be valued in the gold of Ophir In precious onyx or sapphire. Neither gold nor crystal can equal it, Nor can it be exchanged for jewelry of fine gold. No mention shall be made of coral or quartz, For the price of wisdom is above rubies. The topaz of Ethiopia cannot equal it, Nor can it be valued in pure gold. "From where then does wisdom come? And where is the place of understanding? It is hidden from the eyes of all living, And concealed from the birds of the air. Destruction and Death say,'We have heard a report about it with our ears.' God understands its way, And He knows its place. For He looks to the ends of the earth, And sees under the whole heavens, To establish a weight for the wind And apportion the waters by measure. When He made a law for the rain, And a path for the thunderbolt, Then He saw wisdom and declared it; He prepared it, indeed, He searched it out. And to man He said, Behold, the fear of the Lord, that is wisdom, And to depart from evil is understanding.'"

Wisdom has a mysterious nature. Very valuable for a life of success, it cannot be found among the sons men. Where do you find wisdom?? There are four different levels of wisdom.

James 3:15

This wisdom does not descend from above, but is earthly, sensual, demonic.

1. Earthly wisdom = Common sense
2. Sensual wisdom = Receive through sensual experience
3. Demonic wisdom = Occultic
4. Wisdom from above = God's wisdom

Daniel 2:20-23

Daniel answered and said:"Blessed be the name of God forever and ever, For wisdom and might are His. And He changes the times and the seasons; He removes kings and raises up kings; He gives wisdom to the wise And knowledge to those who have understanding.

He reveals deep and secret things; He knows what is in the darkness, And light dwells with Him. "I thank You and praise You, O God of my fathers; You have given me wisdom and might, And have now made known to me what we asked of You, For You have made known to us the king's demand."

Heavenly wisdom connects to divine dominion, God alone provides it. Daniel was unparalleled in his career because he tapped into heavenly wisdom. This wisdom connects you with its true source and causes you to surge beyond your personal effort. Through wisdom your skill becomes refined in your field. You understand deep things concerning your field that you cannot learn through your human efforts.

Daniel 1:17

As for these four young men, God gave them knowledge and skill in all literature and wisdom; and Daniel had understanding in all visions and dreams

Wisdom is a divine gift to the Word lover. God has hidden wisdom from the proud but has made it plain to you, lover of God's Word. Through this wisdom your life becomes a mystery, you cannot be understood, limited or contained. You profoundly break the limit and boundary set by men. Your frequency in divine wisdom depends on the level of your revelation of God's Word. Get to the Word, love the Word, speak the Word, get wisdom and soar on wings as an eagle.

1 Corinthians 2:7

But we speak the wisdom of God in a mystery, the hidden wisdom which God ordained before the ages for our glory

Relationship with God

Romans 16:27

To God, alone wise, be glory through Jesus Christ forever. Amen.

The Lord is glorious, and you are a partaker of divine nature. A constrained and limited life deflects divine glory. Once divinity infuses your humanity, your life becomes glorious. Remember, your relationship with God is your guarantee of a life of perpetual conquest. It is the pillar that holds your wisdom and anchors your soul. Once the relationship with Him is gone, so is the wisdom.

Your relationship with God is the secret behind the unquenchable fire of your divine wisdom. Through your relationship with him, you gain wisdom; you increase in wisdom and you dominate in wisdom.

Cherish and honour your relationship with God above the treasure of the earth by praying, spending time in His word, and consistent fellowship with the brethren of faith. The Almighty is the source of all things. Once you allow your heart to be clouded by any god, you have renounced your divine wisdom. Solomon worshipped other gods than the one who gave him wisdom. The wisest man who ever walked on Earth in the Old Testament turned out to be the most confused man; he called everything vanity. Once you lose your relationship with God, you lose the purpose of life. Guard your relationship and increase in wisdom. Pursue this relationship through growing in your prayer life, Word life, love life and all that concerns the kingdom for you.

Proverbs 3:19

The Lord by wisdom founded the earth; By understanding He established the heavens;

Wisdom is a secret

1.Corinthians 2:7

We speak God's secret wisdom, which he has kept hidden before the world began, God planned this wisdom for our glory.

A secret is a matter concealed from one group while revealed to another. Are you among the concealed or revealed? Become part of the revealed, to walk in the fullness of your destiny. Your destiny is a concealed matter, it is revealed through the virtue of wisdom when you sit under the wings of the Almighty. With the fear of the Lord, you discover your destiny and live a life by design and not from crisis to crisis. Do you fear the Lord? Do you tremble at His Word? You are a qualified recipient of His secrets.

Psalm 25:14

The secret of the Lord is with those who fear Him, and He will show them His covenant

Psalm 103:7 He made known His ways to Moses, His acts to the children of Israel.

CHAPTER 6

Divine Joy

Romans 14:17 says

for the kingdom of God is not eating and drinking, but righteousness and peace and joy in the Holy Spirit.

Joy is a divine force leading to dominion. When you enter a covenant relationship with Jesus, He gives you the Holy Spirit. He is the custodian of joy. It is one of His fruits. The depth of your joy is predicated on your relationship with the Holy Spirit. If you are struggling with joy, check your relationship with Him. The Holy Spirit floods your spirit with joy apart from your natural circumstances. Through the Calvary covenant, you were transported from the kingdom of darkness to the kingdom of light. Joy is the temperament of a kingdom citizen.

The Spirit of God, the chief agent of Kingdom culture, produces the evidence of His presence, joy. You cannot be part of the kingdom and lack joy. God's covenant is a melting pot of the expression of divine abilities.

God's strength is unlimited and available through the virtue of the covenant found in His joy. Without the revelation of divine joy, you will be stranded and isolated on your path to dominion. Joy injects divine strength so that you leap over the obstacles standing between you and the fullness of dominion.

Nehemiah 8:10 says: for the joy of the Lord is your strength.

True conquering and unstoppable joy is from God. It empowers you to live a life of dominion despite challenges. You don't need your situation to change to have joy. Joy sustains you in the most unpleasant circumstances of life. You don't have to wait for the situation to change to celebrate. You can celebrate now! The joy of the Lord is a river that covenant people travel on to the land of dominion.

It is not predicated by the situations of life, it cannot be stopped by diabolical maneuvers. It is not understood by the haughty-minded, but it is Spirit breathed and birthed. Why would Daniel wish for a long life for a king who wanted him dead?

For the Lord prepares a table before you in the presence of your enemy.

Joy is a gift from God to outlast the enemy. When trouble arises from every corner, joy strengthens you from your inner man, sustaining your faith from diabolical arrows and setting you above. Why would Paul and Silas sing in a prison cell? Joy.

You can stir up wells of joy by worshipping and singing praises unto the Lord. Habakkuk endured a devastating situation, but joy anchored him and he was strong during difficult and impossible situations.

> Daniel 6:21 Then Daniel said to the king, "O king, live forever!

> Psalm 23:5 You prepare a table before me in the presence of my enemies; you anoint my head with oil; my cup runs over.

> Acts 16:25 About midnight Paul and Silas

were praying and singing hymns to God

Habakkuk 3:17-19

Though the fig tree may not blossom, Nor fruit be on the vines; Though the labor of the olive may fail, and the fields yield no food;

Though the flock may be cut off from the fold, And there be no herd in the stalls– Yet I will rejoice in the Lord, I will joy in the God of my salvation. The Lord God is my strength; He will make my feet like deer's feet, And He will make me walk on my high hills.

Understanding Divine Timing

Abraham prayed for Sodom and Gomorrah, but God still destroyed these cities. David prayed for his child with Beersheba, but the child died. You are called to exercise your covenant right while dealing with the challenges of life. You ought to accept the divine outcome as the best for you. The ability to wait and accept the divine response is embedded in divine joy. Though we know God's timing is best, waiting is a challenge. Joy infuses your spirit with supernatural contentment, standing against all odds.

Psalm 30:5

For His anger is but for a moment, His favor is for life; Weeping may endure for a night, But joy comes in the morning.

The joy of the Lord is a divine platform that announces you to the nations of the earth. It shelters your faith and incubates your hope. You become single-minded in troublesome situations until your deliverance comes. It lifts you up above the compromising storms of life.

You become steadfast, knowing in whom you have believed; it propels you to a life of excellence shielded from the arrows of depravity. Never try to explain your joy to the naysayers. In trying to explain your joy, you will lose it. Just be joyful. It is contagious. Joy is an act of total confidence in God. Through Divine joy, you become a force to be reckoned with, unbeatable by the enemy weapons. Rejoice!

Philippians 4:4

Rejoice in the Lord always. Again I will say, rejoice!

CHAPTER 7

Divine Peace

Peace is not the absence of war or turmoil, but a person. His name is Jesus. He is the Prince of Peace. The achievement of peace is a response to the invitation of its prince, Jesus. No Jesus, no peace. Lasting durable peace is a heavenly commodity wrapped in a person. The quest for peace starts at the acknowledgment of our human failure to manufacture this precious heavenly substance.

Peace is the abode of the divine, the axe of dominion. It conquers darkness and allows the seed of regeneration to blossom. Without peace, believers are left at the mercy of their circumstances, tossed back and forth by the enemy. Dominion is found in the state of peace, crushing evil forces and causing believers to soar unhindered.

Romans 16:20 says, And the God of peace will crush Satan under your feet shortly.

Peace crushes, it pulverizes the enemy. Satan thrives on the wings of chaos, but once we release Divine Peace, the enemy is paralyzed.

Divine peace is the force of light that cuts through the territory of the enemy. Do you want to defeat the enemy? Walk in the peace of God. God exercises dominion, not as the Lord of hosts, but the God of peace. Peace explains true biblical warfare.

I love leading prayer meetings. Often when we pray, people would seem to be quiet and composed, but when it is warfare time, everyone screams and yells. It seems to me as if he who screams the most pushes the enemy the furthest. This is far from the truth.

This is the truth, your victory is wrapped in peace. The God of peace instructed Israel to walk through the wall of Jericho. Joshua was instructed not to speak while walking around the enemy camp; on the seventh day they shouted, and the wall crumbled. The strength of the shout was rooted in seven days of silence. During chaos, be still and see the salvation of the Lord. When you fight, the Lord keeps quiet and when you are still, the Lord fights for you.

Joshua 6:20

So the people shouted when the priests blew the trumpets. And it happened when the people heard the sound of the trumpet, and the people shouted with a great shout, that the wall fell down flat. Then the people went up into the city, every man straight before him, and they took the city.

Psalm 46:10

Be still, and know that I am God; I will be exalted among the nations, I will be exalted in the earth!

God's peace cannot be explained; it is rooted in His Nature, an invisible axe that cuts through the roots of confusion in the mind and sets your soul at ease. It surpasses human understanding, has to be experienced. The children of Israel had all the reasons to cry out and scream. Pursued by the most powerful army on earth with no means of defense while facing the Red Sea, an insurmountable obstacle. But the Lord demanded for stillness.

Exodus 14:13

And Moses said to the people, "Do not be afraid. Stand still and see the salvation of the Lord, which He will accomplish for you today. For the Egyptians whom you see today, you shall see again no more forever.

In the most impossible situations of life, the remedy is to be still and go forward. Though it sounds like an oxymoron, kingdom progress is made through peace. How long have you been screaming at the enemy?

This is your season to be still and know He is God. The battle is never yours, but the victory is. To access the fullness of Calvary victory, learn to live in divine peace. True peace is not a product of your effort, but a response to your conversation with Jesus Christ.

Philippians 4:6

Be anxious for nothing, but in everything by prayer and supplication, with thanksgiving, let your requests be made known to God;

Christ left you His peace, you have a choice. Either you embrace it to enjoy it or reject it live like a pauper. A victorious life is embedded in the life of peace. Jesus, who is the Prince of Peace, is in you. You have the root, getting ready for the fruit. The life of peace births ever expanding and supernatural realities. Jesus Christ is your peace, trust Him.

John 14:27

Peace I leave with you, My peace I give to you; not as the world gives do I give to you.

Let not your heart be troubled, neither let it be afraid.

A woman lost her only son, conceived after many years of barrenness. She left the dead body home, rode to the man of God, when asked, She responded, all is well!! Jesus is with you, all is well!!

1 Kings 4:23

So he said, "Why are you going to him today? It is neither the New Moon nor the Sabbath."And she said, "It is well."

To walk in peace requires discipline; it is easier to scream, roar and complain, than to walk in peace. Only when we live in peace is God manifested as Jehovah Sabaoth. The Lord of hosts.

I remember as a young boy I was constantly sick, and my gracious mum would weep every day, knowing that any time I could have lost my life. Being a believer, she prayed, fasted and cried, to no avail.

One day, returning from church after she heard a message on the power of peace, she decided not to cry anymore, but to trust God. That was the beginning of my healing after 18 years of pain.

When you complain, grumble and whine, God stops working, but when you enter His Peace, He is unhindered and gets involved. Today decide to enter His peace.

To experience divine rest birthed out of peace, you must cease from your struggles and receive the gift of peace

Hebrews 4:10

For he who has entered His rest has himself also ceased from his works as God did from His.

Isaiah 26:3 says

You will keep him in perfect peace, Whose mind is stayed on you, Because he trusts in You.

Decide to walk in divine peace. Set your mind on God, fix your mind on His Word, rest on Him, refuse to be troubled. Value peace, become addicted to it, be carried by its instruction, for this is your key to victory in the school of dominion.

John 14:1

"Let not your heart be troubled; you believe in God, believe also in me

Psalm 46:10

Be still, and know that I am God;I will be exalted among the nations,I will be exalted in the earth!

Exodus 14:13

And Moses said to the people, "Do not be afraid. Stand still, and see the salvation of the Lord, which He will accomplish for you today. For the Egyptians whom you see today, you shall see again no more forever

This your season to be still and trust the unfailing love of your Father.

CHAPTER 8

Understanding Jesus' Christ Supremacy

The person of Jesus, born in the little countryside town of Bethlehem, with hundreds of prophecies prior to His birth and several fulfilled during His lifetime, is the key to your life of dominion.

Ever since He walked on earth, history changed forever. Born of a woman that He created. Died and resurrected from the dead. Creator who lived like a created. Chief army commander arrested by simple soldiers. Conqueror of death, Hell and the grave.

Defied laws of nature, walked on water, fed thousands with a loaf of bread and fish. Raised the dead, opened the eyes of the blind, cleansed the lepers.

Jesus Christ is unparalleled; He is not from Earth, so cannot be affected by earthly realities. Was not born through human seed so cannot be tainted by human frailties and limitations. He is divine. He is unstoppable. Storms tried to drown Him. Herod tried to kill him, Jews condemned Him, Judas sold Him.

Two thousand years later, He is still alive, worshipped by one third of the world's population, still growing! He is amazing, the master of time, circumstances, events. The commander of the heavenly army, He is the life key holder, above all.

King of Glory, ruler of the universe, visible and invisible. Jesus Christ, the only man born of woman who defeated Satan, He is hell's worst nightmare.

Above All

John 3:31

He who comes from above is above all; he who is of the earth is earthly and speaks of the earth. He who comes from heaven is above all.

First the natural, then the spiritual, the earthly, then the heavenly. Jesus is spiritual and heavenly. Whoever you know, whatever you have known, Jesus is above it all. He has authority and power over all. Your predicament does not have the last your word over your life. Do you know Him? Resolve to Know Him today in the power of His resurrection. The reality of Christ's supremacy is indisputable, beyond argument. The enemy's crafty mind cannot deny the reality of this clear supremacy. Different weapons had to be used against it, that of fear and deception.

> **1 Corinthians 15:46**
>
> However, the spiritual is not first, but the natural, and afterward the spiritual.

> **1.Corinthians 2:8**
>
> which none of the rulers of this age knew; for had they known, they would not have crucified the Lord of glory

The weapon of the ages

> **John 8:44**
>
> You are of your father the devil, and the desires of your father you want to do. He was a murderer from the beginning, and

does not stand in the truth, because there is no truth in him. When he speaks a lie, he speaks from his own resources, for he is a liar and the father of it

The enemy uses deception to instill fear in those who desire the life of dominion. Understand you were created for dominion, and you are to live in its fullness through your relationship with Jesus Christ.

Satan has used the weapon of fear effectively for years. Subsequently, He sees no need to change strategies. The same was used in the garden against Adam and Eve, which is why Satan is currently the illegal steward and custodian of earthly affairs.

The enemy has trapped countless millions, enslaving them in the cage of fear, the majority giving up on their dreams. He has handicapped millions under this fallacy, bound in fear of death. What would you do if nothing could kill you? The enemy's best weapon is fear, but remember, fear is not your portion! Pursue your dream.

God is on your side. He won't disappoint you. Jesus conquered death and the grave, so there is no need to be afraid; live your life with all confidence rooted in Christ. The enemy's onslaught is beneath Christ's supremacy. Jesus is in charge, so why fear?

Jesus in you is supreme above the Satan's opposition.

2 Timothy 1:7

For God has not given us a spirit of fear, but of power and of love and of a sound mind.

From the Root to the Fruit

1 Corinthians 15:55

"O death, where is your victory? O death, where is your sting?"

1 Corinthians 10:13

13 No temptation has overtaken you except such as is common to man; but God is faithful, who will not allow you to be tempted beyond what you are able, but with the temptation will also make the way of escape, that you may be able to bear it.

Christ Jesus lives in you by His Holy Spirit. No longer you, but Christ lives in you. The height to which you soar is predicated by Him. Know him, through Him set your life standard. You are connected to Christ. His position determines yours. His abilities are yours. As He is, so you must be on earth. Not knowing Christ robs you from operating in your full spiritual potential.

Satan will have no trouble when you do anything else, rather than a heart commitment to know Jesus Christ in the power of His resurrection and fellowship of His suffering.

A quest for your full identity in Christ shakes the very core of Satan's kingdom. Your identity is in Christ, to the degree you know Him, you discover yourself. YOU MUST KNOW JESUS CHRIST, not religion, not doctrine, not your church, not your pastor, not your denomination, but Jesus Christ and Him alone crucified.

Philippians 3:9-11

and be found in Him, not having my own righteousness, which *is* from the law, but that which *is* through faith in Christ, the righteousness which is from God by faith; that I may know Him and the power of His resurrection, and the fellowship of His sufferings, being conformed to His death, if, by any means, I may attain to the resurrection from the dead.

Colossians 1:27 says

To them God willed to make known what are the riches of the glory of this mystery among the Gentiles: which is Christ in you, the hope of glory.

Galatians 2:20

I have been crucified with Christ; it is no longer I who live, but Christ lives in me; and the life which I now live in the flesh I live by faith in the Son of God, who loved me and gave Himself for me.

Christ, the song martyrs sang while being eaten alive by lions under Nero's orders. Through the vicissitudes of life, He sustains the soul, became a man so you can live like a son or daughter of God - became poor so you can be rich. He reigns unhindered. His plans cannot be thwarted. His magnificent ways prevail over all. He is the ultimate source of dominion. He is El Elyon, the Most High God.

Once your roots are established in Christ, your fruits will be Christ's. He gives you the Holy Spirit as a gift. Your life is guaranteed, you are a qualified recipient of divine inheritance. The Holy Spirit ensures the manifestation of Christ's life unhindered in all its fullness. Ignorance of the Holy Spirit robs you of the joy of your newfound life in Christ. He is the person, just like Christ. You are not an orphan because He has taken the place of the invisible Christ. He is the undeniable proof that you belong to the heavenly Father; without Christ's Spirit, you are not His.

Romans 8:9

But you are not in the flesh but in the Spirit, if indeed the Spirit of God dwells in you. Now if anyone does not have the Spirit of Christ, he is not His.

The Holy Spirit, divine agent for access. Apart from Him, none can experience the heavenly treasure. So you must believe in Him and learn from Him. Only then will you look like Christ, in word and works.

He is a person. Learn to talk to Him, get to know Him. The journey of a thousand miles starts with one step. Begin the journey with the Spirit of God today.

John 14:16

And I will pray the Father, and He will give you another Helper, that He may abide with you forever.

Romans 8:29

For whom He foreknew, He also predestined to be conformed to the image of His Son, that He might be the firstborn among many brethren.

Acts 2:39

For the promise is to you and to your children, and to all who are afar off, as many as the Lord our God will call."

You can receive the gift of the Holy Spirit today. He is a promise given to believers and their children.

Pray this Prayer

Father, I come to you in the name of Jesus. I have sinned before you. Today I acknowledge the sacrifice of your Son Jesus Christ, which He paid for me on the cross of Calvary. I ask that you grant me the grace to turn from sin today and live for you. Sin can no longer have control over me because of the shed blood of Jesus. I am accepted into your kingdom and restored as your beloved son. Father, I thank you. I am now washed by Christ's blood and am now born again. I am a new creature. My past is over. I am a citizen of the kingdom of God. My eternity is ensured for good. Now fill me with the Holy Spirit of promise, I ask in Jesus' name! Amen!

www.ingramcontent.com/pod-product-compliance
Lightning Source LLC
LaVergne TN
LVHW090116080426
835507LV00040B/955